GOD WEARS MANY SKINS

MYTH AND FOLKLORE OF THE SAMI PEOPLE

JABEZ L. VAN CLEEF

A SPIRITUAL RESOURCE FOR SUSTAINABLE LIVING
POETRY BY JABEZ L. VAN CLEEF

Books by Jabez L. Van Cleef

On Indigenous Cultures and World Religions

All Is Beautiful: The Navajo Creation Story
God Wears Many Skins
He Kumulipo
The Tawasin of Mansur al-Hallaj
The Alchemy of Happiness
The Unstruck Drum of Eternity: Poetry of Kabir
The Song of Confucius
Igbo Singing, and Three Igbo Stories
Nanai and The Quest for the Fire Bird

More Books by Jabez L. Van Cleef

On Mysticism in the Anglican Tradition

The Song of the Cloud of Unknowing
The Song of the Showing of Love
The Song of the Fire of Love

On Human Rights and Civil Disobedience

The Palimpsest of Human Rights
The Song of the Captives
All One Family Sing &
The Birth of Propaganda

Verse Adaptations of Judeo-Christian Texts

Gospels in Verse
The Saxon Gospel
Strength In Trembling
The Book of Ashes
Four Liturgical Plays

Secular Poetry and Fiction

Painkillers
Heaven On Earth
It Rhymes With Breath: Five Stories of Death
Trust Me On This One: Three Stories of Betrayal
Children of Wrath
Left Eye/Right Eye & Into My Belly

A SPIRITUAL RESOURCE FOR SUSTAINABLE LIVING
POETRY BY JABEZ L. VAN CLEEF

Copyright © 2008
Published by Spirit Song Text Publications
20 Pine Avenue, Madison, New Jersey 07940

All rights reserved. No part of this publication may be reproduced, stored in a retrieval system, or transmitted, in any form or by any means, electronic, mechanical, photocopying, recording or otherwise, without the prior permission of the publisher.

Library of Congress Cataloging-in-Publication Data
God Wears Many Skins. English
God Wears Many Skins: Myth & Folklore Of The Sami People,
by Jabez L. Van Cleef
ISBN 1438221894 (paper).
EAN-13 9781438221892.
I. Van Cleef, Jabez L. 1948-   . II. Title
2 4 6 8 9 7 5 3
Printed in the United States of America

GOD WEARS MANY SKINS

MYTH AND FOLKLORE OF THE SAMI PEOPLE

Contents

The Son of the Sun Is Courting
The Daughter of the Giants.
15

The Fox and the Bear.
29

How the Bear Speaks to God.
41

Kari Woodencoat.
55

The Giant Who Did Not Like Bones.
63

Naughty, Naughty Spider!
67

The Boys Who Didn't Get A Magic Cow.
71

The Moon Daughter's Magic.
77

The Magic Singing.
85

Epilogue: The Death of the Sun's Daughter.
121

God Wears Many Skins: An Essay On Sustainability.
125

The Son of the Sun Is Courting
The Daughter of the Giants.

Before time, there were few men there,
And the women were even fewer.
A man put arms around his woman:
Their blood they blended into one.
The mother suckled her offspring,
Gave the child washing, caring, feeding.
The baby kicked and rocked the cradle,
Got his father's strong sinews, muscle,
Got his mother's good sense, balance,
The ancestor of the Sun's own sons.

That's how we heard it came to be.
So it is told even today.
Out beyond the easternmost star,
To the west of moon and sun, there,
You find hilltops of silver and gold,
Stones for the hearth, stones to wear.
The gold sparkles, the silver glimmers:

On the still sea, the mountain appears.
The stars, the sun, and the pale moon
Smile on the cheeks of the mountain.

The boy child launches his vessel,
Takes with him the best men of all.
The wind takes the sails in its hands,
Pushes the boat between islands;
The pegs keep the wooden shell tight,
Its rudder and tiller turn it,
And the south wind guides it, caring,
Way beyond the moon, still changing,
Way beyond the sun's shining ring.
Soon the moon and the sun will be
Like other stars, about to die,
Growing great just before the end,
Glowing ruby-red as they burn.

An entire year they are gone.
The waves break against the boat's skin.
Finally the journey is over,
At the horizon giant's shore.

From far away, your eye can behold
The blind old giant's fair young maid.
She is the blind old man's support.
She washes his clothes by torchlight.
She beats, and rinses, and dries them,
Smoothes them, and folds his shirt for him.
Every day she makes herself sweet,
Puts fragrant grasses by her breast.
Her eye searches the far horizon:
She catches sight of the trav'ling son.

Now does the giant's daughter speak:

"Where do you come from, whom do you seek?
The house of death, the son of the Sun!
Will you be drink for my father?
Drudgery's price for my brothers?
Something good for me to suck on?
Or my brother-in-laws' venison?"
Now does the son of the Sun answer:

"One God shaped from my own father
Flexible sinews and strong arms here;
Blended mother and father together.

A Goddess fed me milk and honey
And nourished my heart with reason.

"Where do I come from, whom do I seek?
Now does the son of the Sun speak:
In the high storm I seek repose,
And a mild smile my wrath dissolves.
In life: someone to gladden me;
In death: a friend; in hardship: a way.
In heartache, I cry for support;
Under burden of need, a comfort.
A mouth to share the catch within,
Someone to guide me in the unknown,
Where children of us both begin."

Their blood began to find its course
As unrest beat in the young breast.
The giant's daughter spoke again.

"Let us two blend our blood within:
Let our hearts be made into one.
In sorrow and joy, father, now bless,
In the name of my mother, bless,
Us in our prayer, sighing and loss.

Son of the Sun, brought by the wind,
I hand you to my father's hand.
Call my mother in sand and birchbark,
Call her from light, call her from dark!"

The giant spoke to his daughter then:

"Let him come in, son of the Sun,
Let us try the strength of our hand,
Let us make and then break this bond.
Finger to finger, stretch our sinews
To know whose flesh will be strongest,
See whose finger will straighten first!"

The giant, vulnerable and blind,
Reaches forth his own shaking hand;
His daughter, protective of her love,
Meets his hand with an iron glove.

The giant spoke to his daughter again:

"Sturdy they are, the hard sinews
Of the Sun's people here with us!
Hard is the young man's finger nail."

For he knew that here he might fail,
And his own daughter would be lost
To this man from faraway coast.

He took fish fat to quench his thirst,
A tar bucket as a courting gift,
And they shared horsemeat for a snack.
The hard skulls filled with mead and glog.
The blind old giant, roaring, drunken,
Pulled and tugged at the gauntlet iron.
The sweat ran down; up rose the heat;
The men grew weaker through the night.

On the hide of the ocean's king,
The whale, underwater sovereign,
In their struggle they lay them down,
Cut wounds in their fingers to the bone.
Hand in hand and chest to chest
Together, their blood in the great force.

The old giant knew then that his loss
Would tie the tangle of their kiss,

And their interlacing agony
Would frighten off knots of envy.

They cut the snare, loosened the band:
And so the wedding party began.
To his spinning wheel, and his bed,
She came, who had twisted sedge thread;
To his steady seamstress, the needle
He gives her, of his own supply.

Up from the shore, out from the earth,
Silver and gold are carried forth.
They've brought the dowry to the boat;
It's filled, so it will scarcely float;
Precious stones above the gunwale:
Gifts to the daughter of this hall,
And him who holds her heart in thrall.

The giant's daughter spoke again.

"Will the boat hold a greater load?
How has the trav'ling swimmer filled?"

Her maiden shoes, she took them off;
Hid well the ancestress rag and cloth;
Giving herself to this strange man,
She clasps his key to her domain.

Three chests from the middle house:
These are what she has carried out.
One is blue, one red, one white;
Three knots there are: for peace and strife,
For blood and fire, for death and life:
From the three gods and goddesses,
Three knots in the cloth she carries.
Now her brothers come from fishing,
Ablaze with walrus and seal killing.
They seek her, they miss their sister.

"Where's the beauty we know from her?"

They find traces of the man there,
On the bed of their own sister,
And quick as light, they ask their father:

"Whose sweaty smell was sweet to her?
Who smelled the smell of our sister?

Who knew the sweet grass of her bosom?
Who took her hand to touch and hold him?
Who showed her manly strength and care,
And plays the manly game with her?
Who teases the young maid in her,
Tenderly strokes the goddess's door?"

And quick as light, the giant answers:

"The son of the Sun, the sailor is."
Anew the brothers take their boat
And pursue the young ones in it.
They labor with their forearms thick,
And all to bring their sister back.
Soon are heard the mighty oar strokes
As the strong boat's timber-skin creaks;
So loud it drowns the waves' own roar.

The giant's daughter, she has no fear,
She unties the maidenhood knot.
The wind grows, bellies the sail out,
Driving their boat quickly forward,
So that the brothers are left behind.
They clutch and hold the pairs of oars

Till they force out hot sweat and tears,
Howls and threats, orders and oaths,
Their gall melts in their very guts,
And their wrath blazes, falls, and seethes.

The giant's daughter's eyes sparkle
At their escape from such a peril;
The young bride's heart hammers out hard,
And she longs for her marital bed.
Her stomach swells, her body spread,
Now forgotten her family's blood.
She casts a glance at her husband:

"Can this boat handle stronger wind?"

So answers her the son of the Sun:

"The mast and rope and sails are strong,
Nothing will sacrifice this boat!"

So then she loosens one more knot
From the fine alder-colored cloth.
Anew, the storm takes hold of them,

Swells the sail of the sea's children.

The brothers, losing another chance,
Boil in their blood, thirst for vengeance,
The last of their strength brought to bear.
Blood and sweat are wiped away clear.
Bent fists, curved backs, touching shoulders,
Their hands are stuck fast to the oars,
Their hearts boil, the boat rushes
And cuts through the sea's water-walls.
And through the eyes made salt-sea blind,
Again they see, they are right behind.

The giant's daughter speaks again:

"Can this boat handle stronger wind?"

She loosens the knot of deliv'rance,
And wrath reaches far beyond humans;
The main servant of the highest god
Reaches down and waves his own hand:
Squalls from the heavens, to the east,
Come as god's wind: they shake the mast;
They tear and shred the sturdy sails.

The boat is tossed between the billows.

The giant's daughter seeks some shelter,
Closes her eyes, crawls down under,
Down to the bottom of the boat.
Sunrise draws near, and in the light,
The brothers are on the lookout.
They have gone ashore, on the land,
Searching for their sister in the open.
When her new father, the Sun, comes,
He sees them with their sharp weapons:
They see the Sun, and they harden,
He has turned their foreheads to stone.
They can still be seen in Vågen;
A copper boat within the mountain.

On bearskin and reindeer doe skin,
Then lay the bride of the Sun's own son.
The bride would now become a Sámi,
Human in size, like you and me.
She took an axe from her own chest
To make her own doors wide and vast
To make a room large as the earth
For the Sun's son's sons; then gave birth.

The Fox and the Bear.

The mountain Sami was driving his sleds.
The fox was wandering in the woods,
And he was hungry, saying in his head,
"What should I do? I'm half-dead!"
Then he came up with this idea:
"I'm going to lie down right here,
Here where the real people come and go,
As if I were dead in the snow."
So he lay down there, as if to die.

The mountain Sami was driving his sleds,
A string of reindeer sleds, through the woods.
He found the fox, frozen stiff, dead,
And threw his corpse on the last sled,
There, with a bunch of frozen fish.
He drove off again into the forest.
The fox came to life, and gnawed away,
The towrope began to weaken and fray,
And finally, the sled came free;
The mountain Sami, he didn't notice

That he had lost his sled of fish.
The fox took the fish, left the sled there
And pretty soon he met the bear.
The bear said, "Where did you get those fish?"
The fox said, "At the real-people's house;
I sat down on top of their well,
And the fish came and bit my tail."
The bear said, "Is that what they do?
Can I make them bite my tail too?"
The fox said to him, "Sure you can,
Just sit, and stick your tail down in!"

Now at that time, long, long ago,
The bear, he had a long tail too.

So the bear went over the hill,
And stuck his tail in the peoples' well.
Some time later he was sitting there,
Waiting for fish in the cold night air,
When the fox came running up to him.
The fox asked the bear, "Where are they?
Aren't the fish biting your tail today?
You'll know, when your tail gets heavy."
The bear said: "I don't really know;

I think it's a little heavy now."
The fox thought, it's not frozen solid yet.
So he sat for an hour or so to wait.
Then suddenly, he began to shout:
"Wake up and bring your spears, real people!
This bear is shitting in your well!"
The bear jerked himself off the hole,
And the force of it ripped off his tail,
Because the ice froze it solid,
And so he ran away without it.

He set out angry after the fox,
And first the fox hid in some rocks,
Then ran under a fir tree root.
The bear began to dig the fox out,
And got hold of him in his jaws,
To carry him to his eating-place.
On the way there, the fox remarked,
"Things were better when I prepared
That feast with all those little birds."
The bear said, "What are you telling me?"
The fox said, "Those were better days
That time I feasted on little birds."
The bear says: "Can't you show me

How to prepare a feast that way?
Can't you dress me up that way too?"
The fox said, "I suppose I can,
But you won't be able to stand
All the pain of preparation,
That those small birds could tolerate."
The bear said, "Oh, I can take it."

The fox said, "You have to do a lot:
First you have to dig a big pit,
Then put a pile of wood in it;
Then pound in pegs, all around;
And twist withes, and be tied and bound;
And finally you start the fire;
You do all this, just to prepare."
The bear said, "Oh, I can do that."
And so he began to dig a pit,
And carried wood to pile up in it,
Then he pounded in pegs around,
And twisted withes, and he laid down;
Then the fox tied him fast in place,
Around his legs, with the withes.
The bear's back was turned toward the pit,
And the fox lit the wood that was in it.

A big flame rose up toward the skies,
The fox began to bite the withes,
He bit them off, the bear fell down
Into the pit and there he burned.

When there was no more smoke or fire,
And only the ashes were left there,
The fox gathered the bear's burnt bones,
And kept them with his possessions.

He dragged them with him in a sack.
The Sami saw the fox coming back.
He was leading his string of reindeer.
He asked the fox, "What do you have there?"
The fox said: "Something precious, and rare;
 My father's and mother's inheritance,
Silver and gold, and large gemstones."
The mountain Sami said to the fox,
"Don't you want to give me that sack?"
The fox said, "No, but I'll swap it."
And so the mountain Sami swapped
His reindeer for the fox's sack.

The fox said, "Now, there is a spell,

Which keeps the things in there valuable.
You must not open the sack up,
Or else the magic will escape!
Wait first, until you have gone
Over five or six small mountains.
If you open it before then,
The treasure will turn into burnt bones."

Then they each went on their own track,
The mountain Sami with the sack,
The fox with the string of reindeer,
Each thinking he had done better.
When the fox had come a long way,
He found some friends who were hungry.
They all began to strike and flay
Those reindeer, for their feasting day.
His comrades were the wolf and crow,
And a weasel, white as the snow.
They took arrows and began to shoot:
First, the wolf shot into the heart,
And to this very day there is
A little narrow bone he has,
That people call the wolf arrow,
Right by where the heart would go.

The weasel shot the second arrow,
Down where the hoof comes to the ground,
And to this very day there is
A little narrow bone he has,
That people call the weasel arrow.

There was no arrow that I know,
That was shot by the black crow.

Then they took care of slaughtering.
And while he stood by there, watching,
The sly fox was always wondering
How he could get it all himself.
It occurred to him, he should try
To get everything in this way:
First he lay down, and he thought,
"I'm going to wash a reindeer gut,
Wash out his stomach in secret!"
Then he began to shriek and groan
As if he were in terrible pain,
As if people had got hold of him,
And were preparing to eat him.
Then his comrades became frightened
And they all ran away, and hid;

Only the weasel secretly stayed.

Then the mountain Sami returned;
When he came, he took a firebrand
And threw it, burning, at the weasel.
He only hit the tip of the tail,
So the weasel's tail tip is black
As the charred wood on the burnt stick.
The fox started to run away
From the mountain Sami that day.
He came to a lake filled with fish;
He stood on a rock at the edge;
And he shouted, "Fish, come ashore!
Come and help! Carry me over,
I don't know how to swim yet!
I'm not supposed to get my feet wet!"

The char came, and it was little.
The fox said: "You are kind and gentle;
But not big enough to carry me."

Then a big fat sea trout came.
The fox said: "You are kind and gentle;
Come in closer to shore, a little,

Then I can get up on your back!"

Sea trout came close, and with a jerk,
The fox grasped it, and pulled it out
Onto the rock where he stood;
He pulled it into the underbrush,
And made a fire to fry the fish.
Soon after, he heard warriors
Coming closer through the forest;
He heard the branches breaking
Below their feet, as they were walking.
He wasn't sure what he was hearing:
He told himself, "That is the song,
Of my fat fish that is cooking."

Nevertheless, when the fox saw
That people were coming still closer,
He grabbed the hot fish mighty quick,
And slapped it hard against a rock.
Then the hot fish fat spattered
So that the fox's eyes got burned,
And the hasty fox became blind.
He began to roam from place to place,
Asking everything he met, for eyes.

He met the birch tree first, and said,
"Can you lend me eyes, for a moment?
I left my eyes by a waterfall
on the other side of this hill.
Lend me yours; you'll get them back
As soon as I find them, I'll return."
The birch wasn't having any of that;
So the fox came to the aspen and said,
"Lend me your eyes for a little while!
I'll give them back, I promise I will!"
The aspen said, "I'll swap mine for yours;
Bring back mine when you have the others."

The fox got new eyes from the aspen,
And the aspen got eyes that were burned.
You know the fox never came back there,
Coming back was not his nature.
Therefore the aspen to this day
Uses these poor burned spots to see;
The burned eyes he got from the fox.
The fox went on, up over the rocks,
And when he went up a high mountain,
I didn't care to follow him,
To see how things went, later on.

The fox just went over the mountain,
And I went back home again.

How the Bear Speaks to God.

The Sami tell how we began
Here on this world that's always been:
Our life, born of the father Sun
And the mother Earth under him.
So have men and women been born
Since the son of the Sun returned.
They have this world in equal share
With reindeer, fish, fox, wolf and bear;
All animals and folk belong
To the same source and becoming.
They are all linked by their spirits
And none of them holds dominance.

Those who believe only one God
Made every thing that is good,
Think of God as something they own.
The Sami see, God wears many skins:
The Sami do not care who owns:
They do not force others to bow:

All the other views may be true.

Since there are many Gods out there,
They need to talk to each other.
Because he was not burdened with fear,
From the first day, we think the bear
Talked often to the sky and air,
Sat with the lord of the mountains,
Governing all the lesser clans;
And from the first day, when he stood,
Held out his arms, stretched them out wide,
We saw the light come 'round his head,
And we showed him our great respect.

We think that every human being
Needs to bring bears an offering.
People give bears the gifts that come
When their own minds abandon them:
When they've been frenzied with delight
They bring of this, some scant remnant,
Scraps from feasting, wounds of romance,
Half-remembered steps in a dance;
They lay these at the door of the cave,
As the best that the bear may have.

They go berserk, as this will mean
They wear a shirt made of bear's skin;
They bow before an ancient Arthur,
A king, known as the bear-hero;
And they concede a certain power,
Because bears can sleep through winter:
The mysterious, half-living sleep
In the stranger, half-worldly deep;
Yet he may wake to live forever.

We find the bones of the dead bear
High up, in the thin mountain air,
Dry and pale gray, under the sky
Where he has come away to die.
The bear is more like people are
Than any other thinking creature:
He stands up on two legs to strike,
With eyes that skewer like a spike,
And when we cut away his skin
He looks like a great bloody man.

All peoples in this land of ice
Where lights dance in the midnight skies,
Give bears some godly qualities,

And ask them to perform some service:
Each one of us gives the bear words
To carry and tell to the Gods.

And we believe that these words are heard
In the right language for a God,
Neither speaker, nor hearer, sure
Whether a meaning's fully there;
Both sides knowing, there are mountains
We climb, to find where heaven is,
And that the bear is in a higher
Meadow than men and women are.

The real people thus have a need
To find in nature, a sort of trade:
The fish and meat we gather here
Come from the good will of the bear;
Because the bear's great vitality
Gives him greater authority:
From this, the bear tells every one
How to come forth with their children,
And how many will yet be born.

We think the bears may live forever,

And yet we know there is anger
In the mind of every bear,
Either from the pain of his death,
Or because in spite of his worth,
His rarity, and likeness to us,
We kill him with spears and arrows,
Make free with his flesh over fires,
And let his spirit nourish us.
He dies before his anger is complete,
And for this we know a great regret.

For these three reasons: respect,
Bargaining, and expiation,
We make for the bear a religion.
Without rightness before the bears
And before all of the others,
We will not know a good hunt,
Our reindeer will not calve nor mount,
We will suffer misery and want.

Today, as we watch the ice melt,
Fresh water turning into salt,
Flocks of birds trying to molt,
The frost under the soil gone soft,

As fish along the shoreline float;
We think back when we felt that need
First, to engage nature in trade.
We have cheated whenever we could;
We have stolen all nature's goods,
And left but little for our own need,
Except if we pay money for it,
And this we sell ourselves to get.

All of the spirit talk and deed
Is gone, but still we know the need.

Behind their eyes, creatures see us
Just as we see them, as creatures.
They breathe and think and do as we,
All living in the same mystery.
They have a language of their own,
And understand words of human,
They have their own big families,
Obey their leaders, bow to their gods.
And while we hunt and kill freely,
Believing it to be necessary,
We know danger when we do it,
And do not think it a light matter;

Because in killing, the hunter
Both gives and receives great anger.

Departure for the Forest.

May the bear hunt now lead us forth
Past the line of light in the south,
While the snow, new or old, sits heavy
Along the branch of the spruce tree.
When we find the den he is in,
Then we will get the drumming man;
All the other hunters will come,
And they will bring their spears with them.
The one who found the bear is leading.
He holds a staff with a brass ring,
And the drumming man follows him,
Then, behind him, are the hunters,
The ones who know killing of bears.

The Hunt.

May the one who first found this bear
Be sent into the creature's lair
To waken it from its slumber.

And may the Sami follow there,
With bow and arrow, lance and spear,
Releasing the spirit of the bear.
And if a spear is in my hand,
May I turn its point backward
Until the bear comes quickly forth
And takes its tip into itself.

Birching the Bear.

After the bear has been killed there,
May they drag it forth from the lair,
And whip it on its back and legs
With birch branches and fragrant twigs.
And may the hunters twist a switch
In the form of a ring, and catch
The lower jaw of the bear with it,
And tie the other end to the belt
Of the leader of bear-killers;
He who pulls at it three times, sings
In his own voice meandering,
That he is now the bear's master,
And that the bear shall follow after.

The Bear Master Returns.

When the hunters return back home,
Their wives all come out to greet them:
They spit bark juice in their faces.
The lead bear-killer advances.
Knocking three times at the hut door.
May he bring the ring into there.
And if the bear is like a woman,
May he call out, "Holy woman!"
And if the bear is like a man,
May he call out, "Holy man!"
The bear master's wife wraps the ring
In linen until after feasting.

The Feast.

May it be proper for the men
To cook the bear meat for feasting
In a special bear-cooking hut,
And may no women enter it.
May the women cover their heads,
Tying scarves over their braids,
And spend the next five days looking

At the bear killer through a ring.
May the bear's skin be stretched out tight
In the center of the banquet,
And may tobacco, foods and drinks
Be left to give its spirit thanks.
And may contrite speech be given
Before the feasting has begun.

Ringing Him In.

After the feast the ring is taken
And the women and the children
Tie some pieces of chain to it:
May the bear's tail then be cut,
And tied to the ring and the chain,
And given to the hunting men;
And may it be buried with the bones.
And may great care now be taken
That the bones are laid as they were
When they were alive in the bear.

Sheltering the Women.

May the skin on a stump be laid

And the wives come with eyes covered,
Blindfolded wives of the bear slayers,
To shoot at the bearskin with arrows.
And may their shooting protect them,
And their children, from what might come
From the dead bear's vengeful spirit.
If they fear, may they conquer it.

May this religion make us secure
From the Sami to the Amur,
And all across Siberia,
As far as far Kamchatka.

A cub is captured in the forest;
Where his mother is made a feast.
Then may the cub be brought to us,
And kept in a cage as he grows.
And during his time among us,
May the cub be our honored guest,
With one person caring for him,
Walking and cleaning and feeding him.

When he has grown into his fulness,
May the cub also make us a feast.

May we make circle, where he will die.
May he be taken from his cage,
And led from hut to hut on leash,
As we tease him with fir branches.
And as we give him reassurance,
May the bear's caretaker secretly
Come near, and kiss him a good-bye.
May the bear be led to a river,
Around the house three times over,
And then be led into the house.
Then may everyone leave the house
Except for the oldest kinsman there.
Finally, may the place of the bear
That has been prepared for it there,
May this place be completely clear,
And the bear tied to two stakes there.
And may the bear be left alone
While all the feasting has begun.

The host must feed the bear also,
The last time, before he will go.
"Farewell, friend," he says to the bear,
"I feed you for the last time here;
Now go back to God your owner.

May you be able to gain favor,
And live in prosperity there."

The village chieftain walks ahead,
Carrying a kettle and a blade;
The medicine man follows him,
Holding in his hands the same.

The bear killer waits for the bear
To turn and reveal the spot where
An arrow will go straight to its heart,
All the while speaking softly to it.

The bear's first body is laid out
On the snow facing toward the west.
All of its skin is taken off it,
But the head is kept intact.
May the head and skin be laid out
On a framework like a body.
May arrows, tobacco, and food
Be laid out beneath the bear's head.
And may the meat all be eaten
Before another sun goes down
And may two dogs also be killed

To honor the bear's spirit
On the day after the feast.

Kari Woodencoat.

There was a King, he had a son;
And a girl worked in his kitchen.
Her coat was made of slabs of wood,
And every day she worked so hard.
Her name was Kari Woodencoat,
And she said, "What do you think of that?"

One Sunday came, and Kari brought
The King's Son his own washwater.
As she shut the door behind her,
He threw some drops of water at her.
Later, when everyone was ready
To go to church and get holy,
Kari said to them: "May I go?"
And all the others answered, "NO!
Stay in the kitchen, mind the dinner.
You'll just have to stay a sinner!"
Cook was afraid that Kari might
Start for the church, just out of spite,

So to keep her at home again,
She emptied out a cask of grain,
Right there on the wide kitchen floor!
She said, "Kari, you have an hour.
Pick up every kernel here!"
Kari Woodencoat called the birds:
They came and hopped on the floorboards;
Together they picked up the grain,
And had a little talk about sin.
Then she got dressed, and went to chapel,
Riding a horse with a copper bridle.
Just when the Pastor said "Amen,"
Kari, she went back out again;
The King's Son followed after her:
"Where do you come from?" he asked her.
"From Washbasin Land!" she made answer.

Guess what? Sunday came again!
Now Kari brought to the King's Son
A hand-towel as white as the snow.
Just as she was turning to go,
The King's Son threw the towel at her.
She ran downstairs with a clatter.
When off to church the King's Son went,

Again asked Kari Woodencoat:
"May I go to chapel today?"
"NO! Stay here! Cook while you pray!"
And cook took the same cask of grain
And spread it on the floor again.
So Kari called the birds to help;
Together they picked the spilt grain up.
Again she dressed herself for Church.
Her horse now had a silver bridle,
And she had silver clasps as well.

When she came into the chapel,
The King's Son went into a fuddle,
He had no time then to listen
To the Pastor's boring sermon.
He sat and stared at her again.
Just as the Pastor said "Amen,"
Kari Woodencoat went back out,
The King's own Son in hot pursuit.
He could not stop her in her haste.
She climbed into a grand carriage
With four horses ready to charge.
Then the King's Son called after her:
"Where do you come from? Who lives there?"

"From Hand-Towel Land!" Kari said.

When the people got back from Church,
There was Kari in the kitchen,
Clattering in her wooden boards,
And talking again to the birds.
You know what? The third Sunday came!
Kari Woodencoat took the comb
Upstairs to give to the King's Son.
Just as she closed the door behind,
The King's Son opened the door again
And threw the comb at her apron.
Things were busy in the kitchen;
Yet again, it was time for church.
Even cook was ready to go.
And Kari said: "May I go, too?"
"NO!" they said, "You must stay here,
In the kitchen, and mind the dinner!"
The Cook emptied the cask of grain.
Kari got down on her knees again.
She called her little birds to help,
Together they picked all the grain up.
She went to dress herself again,
And now her horse had a golden rein.

And she herself had a golden dress,
And on her feet wore golden shoes.

When she went into church that day,
The room was dazzled by the ray,
Dressed all in gold, there Kari was!
The Pastor said "Amen," and "Bless,"
And the golden girl went back out,
With the King's Son in hot pursuit.
Before the carriage felt her foot,
He reached and seized ahold of it.
Getting himself one golden shoe
Was all that he could ever do.
Before the horses trampled him,
He asked again from where she came.
"From Comb Land!" was her quick reply.
When they got home, there was Kari
In the kitchen, dressed in her boards,
Still conversing with the birds.

Then the King's Son made his father
Write to all kingdoms everywhere,
Looking for Washbasin Land.
"NO!" Came the answer back to them.

Then the King's Son made his father
Write to all kingdoms everywhere,
Looking for Hand-Towel Land.
"NO!" Came the answer back to them.
Then the King's Son made his father
Write to all kingdoms everywhere,
Looking for Comb Land.
"NO!" Came the answer back to them.
Then he got all the women to put
The golden shoe onto their foot.
"HA! HA! It fitted none of them!"

For this gold shoe, so small the foot!
The cook chopped off her toes and heel,
And tried the golden shoe as well.
The birds cried out as they flew by,
"The toes chopped off! Bye bye, bye bye!
The heel sliced off! Bye bye, bye bye!
The golden shoe's all full of blood!
Look for the girl all dressed in wood!"

Then at the last the Cook called back:
"Give me those birds to chop and hack!"
They came to Kari Woodencoat

To try the shoe on her small foot:
What marvel! See the joy of it!
At last, someone the shoe would fit.

The Giant Who Did Not Like Bones.

Once some Real People children took
A little boat across the lake.
Over the lake a mountain stood,
And a great mountain cave beckoned,
So the children could not restrain
Themselves from rowing the boat in.
A giant had his dwelling there:
He was not a friendly fellow,
He was a Man-Eating Stallo.

The children knew nothing of this.
They filled the cave with their shrill cries,
Hearing the echo of their voices,
And the giant heard all of this.
He came down to take a good look.
The children rowed back to the lake,
So he chased them along the shore
And hid behind a big stone there.
He began to call out to them.

They had never heard about him;
They thought they knew the voice they heard,
They headed toward it, rowing hard.

Just as the boat touched the land,
Up popped the Giant! With his hand,
He put the boat up on his back,
And disappeared behind the rock!
All this happened before the children
Could even think of escaping.
The giant was so tall and wide
That his back and shoulders brushed
The highest branches of the trees.
The children caught hold of the branches
And clinging to the prickly needles,
Hung far above, like small birds' nests;
But now the danger, and the terror
Of their being eaten, was over!

When the giant came back home again,
He called his wife into the kitchen.

On the kitchen table he set
The boat with the children, and said,

"Here! Choose a child that's fine and fat,
I want something greasy to eat!"
But the wife of the giant asked,
"Are these the only two you caught?"
"Are you crazy?" cried the Giant;

But when he looked inside the boat,
Only the puniest children were there,
A little boy and his tiny sister,
And they were so weakly, pale and thin!
Their bones were showing through the skin!
Before anyone could eat them,
They had to get some fat on them.

The giant's wife put these two children
Behind bars in a wooden pen.
She brought them delicious food,
Roasted and baked, on plates of gold,
And she told them to eat it.
But they both knew what that meant.
They told each other not to stuff:
Just eat enough to keep alive.
Better to starve than to be eaten,
They said to each other, these children.

One day the giant had a guest,
Whom he wanted to feed the best.
He went down to the children's pen
And found them still thin and bony.
At this he was filled with anger,
And called his wife to yell at her:
"This boy is as thin as a crow,
And the girl is thin as a stick!"

He slung both children on his back,
And carried them down the forest track,
Until he reached their parents' hut.
He threw them inside, roaring out:
"Here! Take your miserable brats!
Such bony creatures, not fit to eat!"
Off he ran through the dark forest
So the earth shook under his feet.

Naughty, Naughty Spider!

BUZZ! Buzz! Buzz! Listen! Swarming gnats!
When the sun burns hot, days and nights,
The real people children suffer
And it's all because of the spider!
In old days there were no mosquitoes.
Far away, beyond southern seas
They heard mosquitoes whine and buzz,
You could see them sucking their suppers,
The people itching all over themselves.
But in the north the real people
Never had this kind of trouble.

One day the mosquitoes of the south
Began to talk of flying north,
For they had heard so much of it
From a spider, that got about,
And had told them of its wonders.
How the cuckoos sang their sweet songs,
The berries ripened, the flowers bloomed!
Walking feasts were all about them,

The reindeer with their juicy skin,
Dogs and goats and little children,
Creatures with no place to hide in;
Sleeping outside with their bare legs!
And there were such nice wet bogs
Waiting for the mosquitoes' eggs.
And the sun shone night and day,
So that the mosquitoes could play
And always find lots of red food.

The spider did not tell them about
The season of long, freezing night,
When the sun would never come out!
Nor did the spider say: "My nets,
Such fine nets as the spider spins,
Out there among the loose stones,
On the shore, where the water comes,
Where mosquitoes do not see them!"

Oh yes! Those mosquitoes of the south!
How they longed to be in the north!
But the Mother Mosquito said:
"First, let's send some scouts ahead,
We'll see just what that land is like."

Six went. And two got safely back.

A reindeer whisked one with his tail,
Another fell in a milking pail,
A third was smothered by tent-smoke,
A fourth was killed by an old man's smack.

The two that came back home again
Said that the north was really fine.

So the Mother Mosquito said:
"Let the gnats go on ahead,
We will stay on here for a while."
But the two said, "It will be well,
If all the mosquitoes go together,
Flying north in summer weather,
All the mosquitoes in a great swarm
Flying north when the weather is warm."
Oh yes! And here they are today,
When the sun burns up in the sky—
Swarms of them, like dark moving clouds:
They come after us around our heads!

Oh yes! And the sweet spider spins

And spins and spins, preparations,
Fine nets among the loose shore stones,
Where the mosquitoes cannot see
The nets, arranged so artfully;
So, the spider suspends her threads
She catches them! And bites off their heads!

The Boys Who Didn't Get A Magic Cow.

ONCE it was in the land of night,
The far off land of Northern Light,
Where the rich real-people kings
Followed the reindeer wanderings—
Pack reindeer, mother reindeer, pretty fawns—
It was a summer day, that once—
Sun ever-shining, sun ever hot,
The king, with his whole wide company,
Came to a valley, wide and green,
And they drove all the reindeer in;
The reindeer grazed on grass so thick,
The men took off the reindeers' pack
And set up tents close to a rock.
The women hung their cooking pot
Over the smoldering fire of peat,
And began to boil reindeer meat.
None of these people knew this place
Was holy for making sacrifice
To a Seite, spirit of stone,
A marker of gods dwelling within;

Whose strange and fearful majesty
Was in a shape they could not see
On the side of the rock they were,
But was apparent on the other.
The Seite belonged to a great wizard,
Who took life from life, out inward.
When he wanted to get your magic,
Wicked spirits would help him make
Evil, and put it on you quick!

He chose a fine white reindeer-buck
Out of the herd, and covered it thick,
With decorations, front and back—
Antlers, legs, flanks, and head,
Every known color of thread,
Yellow, blue, green, and red,
Red-brown, white, gray and black,
Every color, on his long back.
When the buck was adorned just so,
Then it knew just where to go.
It led the way to the Seite,
And the great wizard followed it
There the Wizard killed the buck,
Skewered a chunk of meat on a stick,

And ate it, showing reverence;
They took the meat off of its bones,
And then they cast its bones and horns
On a midden of bones and antlers
Nearby the Seite's sacred stone.
In this way the great wizard got
All the magic power he wanted,
His power the same as the Seite's,
To bring revenge on enemies.

As the real people settled
By the stone, with their reindeer herd,
Nearby, in the king's tent-chamber
Were two boys, traveling together.
Night came on, though the sun still shone,
Neither night nor day, set the sun.
The two boys, for some unknown cause,
Could not pass beyond sleep's doors.
By and by they heard some voices
And looked out into shadowy places,
Where the sunlight coming sideways
Made the rocks seem strange and formless;
They knew then, that this place they'd come,
Where the rocks melted, was the home

Of some Ulda Spirit People.
The boys peeped out again and saw
A whole herd of magic reindeer cows.
They were white and had no antlers.
And the boys knew there was a spell,
That if they threw a piece of steel
Over the herd of magic deer,
They could take one and keep her.
That would bring good luck and riches!
But before they throw it, she vanishes.

This is what happened on those nights,
In the land of the Northern Lights!
Knowing that Ulda Spirit People
Will carry off children, real people
Give all their children amulets
Of copper, or silver, or brass,
To frighten away the Uldas.
Once a real people mother forgot
To give her baby an amulet.
One day she saw that her baby
Was behaving in a strange way.
She knew then that Ulda Spirits
Had taken her child to their haunts,

And had left a changeling instead.
An old real people woman said:
"You must whip that changeling hard:
First, put her in a room that's locked,
And set a small plate of gruel
With many spoons, out on the table,
Then you shall see what you shall see!"
The mother shut the child away,
With a dish of gruel ever so tiny
And many spoons beside it lay.
She heard the child through the keyhole say:

> *I've lived as long as the dwarf birches,*
> *I've lived as long as mountain birches:*
> *Never have I seen such doings!*
> *Many spoons and little porridge!*

Then the Mother knew for sure,
Her real child had been taken from her.
She rushed in and whipped the girl, hard—
She whipped, and whipped, and whipped her—
Beat her, and beat her, and beat her!
Then she locked the changeling in
All by itself, all the afternoon.

And as the evening light grew dim,
She set a burning lamp in the room.

By and by she heard some voices,
The speaking of the Ulda Spirits:
"O woe is far, and woe is near,
They have been beating our Old Mother!"
So said the voices to each other.
"We cannot stand this any more!"
And so when the real people Mother
Got courage to open the door,
It was her own child that she found,
Home again, and safe and sound.
The Uldas took away their Old Mother!
You may be sure the real people Mother,
When she could, as quick as ever,
Gave her baby a charm of silver,
Hid a knife, right in its cradle,
Fastened her with a silver toggle,
Hung many a charm and amulet,
From top of cradle to its foot.
So that whatever came to pass,
She would scare off the evil Uldas.

The Moon Daughter's Magic.

Far back in the age before this,
When the woodcock had white feathers,
And the blackbird was gray as dawn,
And earth was courted by the sun;
Before there were mosquitoes and gnats,
Then there lived two mighty Wizards:
They were named Torajas and Karkias.
Each had his own hunting ground,
And his own place to graze his herd.
A wide lake lay between these two.

They were great Wizards, this we know:
The Spirit of the Magic Drum, Tonto,
Had given them his powers of magic,
Had taught them many Spells to speak,
Forward and backward and upside down,
And to undo the Spells they had done.
These two could race invisibly
Like the Storm Wind across the sky.
They could fly and dip and soar,

Like eagles above the far seashore.
They could be serpents in the sand,
Fleet reindeer running on the land,
Tossing and clashing their broad antlers,
Skimming over the snow-pastures;
To be what they would become,
The Wizards beat their Magic Drums,
Chanted their Spells into the skies,
And each becomes just what he wills.

Karkias had only fair signs
Painted on his magic drumskins.
He never used his skill for harm
Or made someone a slave to him.
But Torajas had on his drum,
Not only good, but greedy scrim.
Great gods had taught the Wizards, yet
Gave them the choice how to use it.
The greedy signs, Black Magic, were
Learned from the Wicked Moon Daughter.

Things were going well on the earth,
Among the brown men of the north.
Their fat herds of tame reindeer

Every day were growing larger.
Their hunting and fishing were good.
They went to Karkias to ask his aid.
They were very rich and happy.

Now down in the dark Underworld,
The Wicked Moon Daughter waited.
Her hair, all coarse and matted
Covered her caved in forehead.
Her long yellow teeth were gleaming
Opening her mouth, grimacing,
She wailed her incapacity,
Because the real people were happy.
So quickly she transfigured,
Into a yellow-eyed Blackbird,
And flew to the tent of Torajas.
And she perched there on the branches
Of a pine tree near his tent door,
And sang a song, mournful and clear:

> *The north's Wizards, they are mighty!*
> *And famed for skill and artistry.*
> *Torajas beats his Drum with cunning.*
> *Marked with Black Art, his drumming!*

Karkias is wise and strong,
Filled with age-old Magic song;
Great his enchantment and his Spell.
Which is greater, which more powerful?
Karkias, or strong Torajas?
So do all real-people ask us!

Thus sang the Wicked Moon Daughter
Appearing as a bird, by the tent-door.
The proud Torajas heard her song,
And in his heart began to long
To be known as the greatest Wizard.
Did Karkias know more spells than he did?
Surely the signs on Karkias' Drum
However they may have come,
Where not as beautiful as those,
That he, Torajas, had on his!
Looking into Torajas' heart,
The Wicked Moon Daughter saw that
Her song had moved him to envy.
She flapped her black wings to fly,
Down from the branches on the wing,
And she sat by his door, and sang:

Let all the north people attend:
Which one is the greater Wizard?
Have a contest between you,
See who the Chief Wizard will be!

At this Torajas' heart was full
With the darkest kind of evil;
And the Blackbird, flapping her wings,
Flew croaking down her dark caverns,
Calling hoarsely to the stone halls
Of the Underland where she dwells.
Her song still rang in Torajas' ears.
Hateful thoughts drove out his joys.
The darkness of the Underworld
There in his heart slowly unfurled.
Envy and bitterness against Karkias
Took root in his mind like big trees!

Through the endless empty days,
Hatred clouded his covetous eyes;
One morning he stood by the water
And he watched Karkias rowing there.
Torajas muttered a dark Spell,
And straightway, storm spirits fell

Like bitter rain, over the lake,
Wind lashing the billows high,
And before Karkias could reply,
The wind lifted the frail raft up,
And cracked the air like a great whip!
Karkias fell down in the lake,
He changed himself to a minnow quick,
And he swam towards the shallows,
But Torajas muttered another Spell:
Suddenly, there came a huge pike
The grandfather of the whole lake,
To devour Karkias, once and for all!
And the pike swallowed him down whole.

Then all the people grieved for him,
Saying, "Throughout all the kingdom,
Karkias was the greatest of Wizards!"
Twelve months went by. Afterwards,
Around the tent of Torajas flew
The Spirit Blackbird, croaking so:

> *Who is the greatest of all Wizards?*
> *The vanished one, Karkias?*
> *Or the fearless one, Torajas?*

Torajas' heart grew foul and black.
Chanting songs of Black Magic,
He set his net out in the lake.
The next day, when he drew the net,
There was nothing but minnows in it.
The next day the net stretched out
Across the lake from side to side.
In the morning, when he looked,
There were some larger fish in it.
He called on the Moon Daughter,
And again he put out his net.
And see! Next morning he pulled it,
The huge pike was in the middle of it,
The grandfather of the lake;
Torajas took up the pike,
And carried it into the village,
Standing among the whole village,
He plunged his knife into its gut,
Thinking, of course, he would kill it.

See! Out stepped Karkias!
As well and whole as he ever was!
"Evil Torajas!" he accused,

"You did me great wrong so to use
Your Black Magic against me thus."
When the people heard all this,
They cried out, "Torajas is greedy,
We will not use his wizardry:
We know Karkias is the greatest,
And he is worthy of our trust."
Raging and fuming, Torajas went
Back to his side of the lake again.
And no one ever came to him,
To ask him for his help again.
But the Moon Daughter cried her cry,
There about his tent, in her tree.
And every time she flapped her wings,
Mosquitoes, stinging and singing,
And biting gnats, buzzing and mad,
Filled the air with a cloud of blood.

The Magic Singing.

Listen to the red haired singer
From the land of thousand waters!

In the days of Golden Wonders,
When the world was like a great egg,
Holding earth and sky there, so big,
The earth down in the lower half,
The sky up in the upper half,
The moonshine glist'ning like the white,
The sunshine blazing yellow light;
There was a great old Wizard then,
Whose name was Vainamoinen:
He came into the Land of Heroes
Out of the rolling, tossing billows,
Out of the white-wreathed foaming waves,
Out of the crested seafoam, rose
The singer of such compelling voice,
The mysterious great enchanter was
High on the wide desolate isles.
We could see him from far at sea,

And his voice echoed off the sky.

He called from earth a Magic Youth
And bade him sow seed by the path,
And seed of many kinds he sowed,
The Magic Youth with fertile seed,
In swamp and lowland, mountain, hill.
Fir trees sprang up around us all,
Birches in swamps, pine trees on hills,
And lindens by the valley trails.
Junipers, hung with clust'ring berries.
All across the Land of Heroes,
Wide, wide forests, flow'ry meadows.
Merry thrushes among the trees,
Trilling velvet-throated cuckoos,
Down among the silver birches.
Strawberries and sweet cloudberries
Luscious and dewy among their leaves.
Golden flowers across the meads:
How lovely were the watery Lands!
Then the wise one, Vainamoinen,
Had his Belt of Wonder Tales on,
Helped us happily pass the day,
With story, on story, on story.

From far away we heard his voice,
All people in the Land of Heroes,
Heard his Magic Songs and stories,
From end of south to end of north,
Everywhere in the whole earth.

In a far, dismal, northern fjord,
Dwelt Youkahainen, a young Wizard.

He heard all the people there say:
"The sweet one of the Land of Heroes,
Is better skilled in Magic Tales
Than our Youkahainen is."

And in that moment, black envy
Entered Youkahainen's body.
"I will go to the Land of Heroes!"
He cried aloud with great purpose.
"I will challenge this other one
To a contest of Wizarding.
I will sing him my oldest tales
And chant my powerful magic spells.
And I will put this one to shame,
Transform him into something mean.

He shall croak like a fat frog,
Being squashed under a big log!"

Youkahainen rushed to his barn,
And led out his ferocious stallion.
Flame darted from its blood red nostril.
Its hoof struck the stone like an anvil.
He hitched his horse to a golden sled,
And, leaping up, took his dog beside.
He struck the horse with the birch whip,
Adorned with pearl along its grip.
Away they sped and the hooves thundered.
All that day they galloped southward,
All the next day, onward and onward.
On the third day, Youkahainen
Arrived by the heath-covered mountain
Where dwelt noble Vainamoinen
High above the Land of Heroes.

Now it happened the ancient was
Driving in his own golden sledge,
Vainamoinen traveled that ridge,
Racing along the wide roadway.
Youkahainen saw him coming,

And did not turn away from him.
Fiercely, he urged his sweating horse
Into Vainamoinen's course!
Two sledges struck like the thunder!
Their shafts were driven together.
The traces were tangled awry,
The horses stood smoking and fiery.

"Who are you, where do you come from?"
Cried the ancient Vainamoinen.
"Your driving is wild and churlish,
And you have broken my best sledge,
And ruined my reins and traces."
"I am the Wizard, young and wise,"
Sneered Youkahainen in his face.
"And what manner of person are you,
Where do you come from and go?
Can it be you're the famous one?
Wizard, Singer, Vainamoinen?
If so, let us sing together,
And show who is the sweeter Singer;
Whoever makes better song today
Shall be the one to keep the roadway.
The other one shall take the edge."

"Youngster, I accept your challenge,"
Said the ancient Vainamoinen.
"But first tell me, if you can say,
Some of the wisest things you know."
Clever Youkahainen answered
"Although I am not yet so old,
I think my wisdom's great indeed!
Here are some of the things I know:

> *Every roof must have a chimney,*
> *Lives of seals are free and merry.*
> *Every fireplace has a hearthstone.*
> *Salmon eat the perch and whiting.*
> *Leave off working when you drink beer.*
> *My people plow the land with reindeer.*
> *In your land they plow with horses.*
> *Such great wisdom shows in faces!*

Said the ancient Vainamoinen,
"Such foolish stuff as you are saying,
May suit the minds of babes and children,
But not of heroes and of great men.
What happened when the world began?"

Again he boasted, Youkahainen,
"Well I know about such wisdom,
I'll tell you all about it: Listen!"

> *Boiling water is malicious.*
> *Fire is full of danger vicious.*
> *Magic is the child of seafoam.*
> *Waters gush from every mountain.*
> *Fir trees were the first of houses;*
> *Hollow stones, the first of kettles.*

"Foolish words!" cried Vainamoinen.
"Is that all you can talk, that nonsense?"

"O I can tell what really happened
In those golden first days back then,"
So said Youkahainen: "Listen!"

> *For 'twas I who plowed the ocean;*
> *Hollowed out the depths of ocean;*
> *When I dug the salmon grotto,*
> *When I all the lakes had made so,*
> *When I put the mountains round them,*
> *When I piled the rocks around them.*

I was present as a hero,
When the heavens were created,
When the sky was crystal-pillared,
When was arched the beauteous rainbow,
When the silver sun was planted,
And with stars the heav'ns were sprinkled.

"Shameless liar!" cried Vainamoinen.
"Prince of all liars that have been!"
"Come, old Wizard!" said Youkahainen,
Tossing his black hair back again.
"Let us fight with knives and spirit!
And if you are afraid to fight,
Then I will sing you to your rest,
Into a wild boar of the forest,
With swinish snout and heart more swinish!"

Vainamoinen's terrible rage
Blazed down fiercely from his visage.
Then he began his Magic Singing,
His Magic Incantations beginning.
Grandly sang wise Vainamoinen,

Sang till shook with fear the mountain,
And the flinty rocks and ledges
Heard his tune and crumbled ridges,
And the gray billows heaved the more
And crashed and thundered on the shore.

So the boastful Youkahainen
Stood still in terror of the old man,
While Vainamoinen sang and sang,
The curves of tune and trilling splendors
Made saplings of the youth's sledge-runners;
His tack and harness turned to alders,
The old man sang the golden sled
Upon the lake, a lily pad;
The birch-whip, all pearl-ornamented,
Suddenly turned into a reed;
And the horse, with hooves of thunder,
To a white stone by the water.

The grand old man Vainamoinen
Sang as if he would never end;
Sang Youkahainen's golden dagger
Into a gleam of lightning jagged,
Across the summer sky above him.

So he disarmed Youkahainen:
Made a rainbow of his crossbow;
Turned to hawks his feathered arrows,
His dog into a block of stone;
His cap was off his forehead flown,
Sung into pieces of white cloud;
His gloves turned into water lilies,
And his wide belt, all set with jewels,
Sung to a twinkling band of stars,
Floating in air around his ears.

As Vainamoinen sang some more,
Youkahainen sank down right there,
Into a swamp of mud and water;
To his waist he had gone under.
He could no longer lift his feet,
Through his body, the great pains shot;
"O wise Vainamoinen!" he cried,
In terror at what he had started;
"O you the greatest of all Wizards!
Speak your Magic Words now backwards,
And free me from this place of horror.
I will pay you what you ask for!"

"What little ransom can you give me?"
Asked Vainamoinen, spitefully.
"If I cease my right Enchantment,
If I free you from this torment?"

"Free me now," cried Youkahainen,
"I will give you for your hunting
Two Magic Crossbows from my house."

"I do not want your Magic Crossbows.
I have bows hanging everywhere,
Hanging on every nail and rafter."

Then Vainamoinen sang some more,
And Youkahainen sank in deeper,
Till he was stuck, down to his shoulder,
In the mud and in the water.

"Oh, I will give you Magic Boats,
Swift and beautiful are their sails!"

"I do not want your Magic Boats.
My bays are full of Wonder Boats."

Then Vainamoinen sang some more,
And Youkahainen sank in deeper,
Till he was stuck in to his chin, there,
In the mud and in the water.

"Please, O Vainamoinen, Please!
I will give you my Magic Horses!"

"I do not want your Magic Horses.
Magic Horses crowd my stables."

Deeper, deeper, down, down, down,
Sank in the mud, poor Youkahainen,
To his shoulders, then to his chin,
Then to where the sweet air came in.

He pleaded then, poor Youkahainen:
He offered the gold that would glisten
In the bright eternal sunshine,
And the silver that would gleam,
In the moonshine's changeable beam,
All his cornfields and all his corn.
But, laden with sorrow and forlorn,
He sank more, even past his chin.

Seaweed filled his nostrils then,
And the grass in his teeth, between.

"O, you ancient Vainamoinen!"
Prayed and beseeched then, Youkahainen.
"Wisest of all wisdom-singers!
Put your Magic now in reverse!
Turn away your Magic weapon!
Save me from this smothering torment!
Free my eyes from mud and torture.
I will give you my Sister Aino,
Fairest of all the north's daughters!
She shall be your own bride and spouse!
To sweep your rooms and keep your house.
She shall rinse your golden platters,
Weave for your bed golden covers.
She shall bake your honey-biscuit
And spread her own honey on it."

"That is the ransom that I wish!"
Said Vainamoinen in a rush.
"The northland's young and fairest daughter
To be my lovely bride forever,

And the pride of the Land of Heroes,
And the greatest of all Wizards!"
Then joyfully, Vainamoinen
Upon a nearby rock he sat down,
Sang a little, then sang again,
And then he sang for the third time.
Backwards he weaved his Incantation,
And backwards sang his Magic Songs.
Suddenly, the charm was broken!
Youkahainen dragged up his feet
From water and mud pulled them out,
Wiped the mud from under his chin,
And stood up like a man again.
He led his horse away from there,
Drew his sledge out of the water,
Found his pearl handled birch-whip,
Hitched his horse and his sledge up,
Threw himself in the front of it,
And sped away with a heavy heart.

Night and day the horse ran strong,
On the third day in the morning,
Youkahainen reached his home.
Still angered from the smell of doom,

He drove reckless against the wall,
Fell out, and stumbled into his hall,
Leaving his smashed golden sledge
In front of the house, by a hedge.

His Mother, gray, withered, and aged,
Came out to meet him in his rage.
"Why do you break your snow-sledge, son?"
Cried his Father, filled with concern.
"Why do you come home this wild way?"
Youkahainen began to weep and cry,
Broken-hearted, after his journey.
"Tell me, First-born, why do you grieve?"
Asked his Mother, touching his sleeve.
"Golden Mother, O faithful one!"
So cried Youkahainen.
"Surely I have good cause to weep.
I have given my own Sister up,
I have bartered your beloved Aino,
To the Wizard Vainamoinen!
Now she must travel to his side,
So he, the Land of Heroes' Pride,
Will wed and take her for his bride!"

His Mother clapped her hands with joy.
But not so, the beautiful Aino,
The fair and darling Maiden fell
Into a passion sorrowful,
And bitter weeping wailed through the hall.

Aino, still shedding her bitter tears,
Then clad herself in fine blue robes,
Adorned her head with silver and gold,
Girded herself with a golden girdle,
And she tied bands, blue and scarlet,
Over her hair and about her forehead.
Then she wandered hither and yon;
For three long days she wandered on,
Singing sadly, muttering madly,
Till at the end of the third day
She reached a bank of purple flowers,
Where the blue lake met the meadows.

And there she hung her robes of blue
On an alder, standing nearby,
And her ribbons scarlet and blue
On an aspen, standing nearby,
And down she sat a while, to think,

On a large, many-colored rock;
As the water surged and relented,
He grieving wailed and lamented.
Then suddenly the large rock sank
Down to the bottom of the lake,
And the lovely Maiden Aino
Down there became a Water-Maiden
In the dark grottoes of the Lake King.
There in the form of a water-salmon
To and fro in the waves she swam.

Now it happened that Vainamoinen
Far in the south though he may have been,
Heard of the wondrous water-salmon,
Set out to catch and bring the fish in.
Day after day, in his copper boat,
He went abroad to look for it,
But for that fish he fished in vain,
With his copper rod and golden line.
Although he caught the salmon once,
It slipped away right through his fingers
Into the water, and swam away.
And a voice cried out, mockingly,
As Aino, in her fish-shape, heaves,

Lifting her head above the waves:

> *"O Vainamoinen, O pitiful!*
> *You have not the wit to hold me!*
> *I am the Water King's darling one,*
> *The Daughter of the son of the Sun!"*

Then turning away, she dived down deep,
The lake's deep water swallowed her up,
And she was never seen again,
Not by old Vainamoinen.

With sorrowful sighs and shaking hand,
He guided his copper boat to land.

After many days had passed,
Lonely and still grief-possessed.
He thought, "I will fish no more here,
I will go try to find her there,
Far in the dismal, distant north,
And if she's not found in this earth,
Then I will seek the Rainbow Maiden
For my bride among all women.
She, the most beautiful of all Maidens,

Dwells on a Magic Rainbow balance."

So to the land of cruel winter,
Vainamoinen, the great singer;
So to the land of little sunshine,
He rides his Magic Dappled Steed on,
Plunging onward, without ending,
Towards the dismal, Northern land.
Onward the Magic Dappled Steed came,
Till they saw the blue water's gleam.
Over the water, he saw it coming,
There was the boastful Youkahainen,
Brash and youthful, greedy Wizard,
Saw the horse of Vainamoinen
Out upon the blue waves skimming,
And he raised his Magic Crossbow,
Drew the cruel bow-string back so,
And he let loose a feathered arrow.

Fast sped the arrow, through the bright air,
Struck the Magic Dappled Steed there,
Passed through Vainamoinen's shoulder.
So headlong down into the sea
Plunged Vainamoinen heedlessly;

Then the boastful Youkahainen
Said, "Vainamoincn's dead and gone!"
And hurried homeward, boasting loudly.
But the rolling waves of the sea
Upheld the ancient Wizard that day,
He swam as if he had a fish fin,
And floated like a branch of aspen.
He swam six days in summer sunlight,
And six nights in golden moonlight.
Then there rose a mighty Wind Storm,
An eagle soaring around his head came:
On its back, the eagle took him
To the far coast and set him down,
Then the great eagle flew away.
And Vainamoinen, old and lonely,
Sat down beside the shore blue sea,
And fell to weeping, long and hard:
For three long days he wept and cried.

Now it chanced, the Rainbow Maiden,
Rosy and beautiful, the virgin,
Went out early in the morning,
Six white fleeces to gather in,
From six gentle lambkins taken,

To make a robe of softest raiment.
She heard a wailing from the water,
And a weeping from the seashore,
She heard a hero's voice lamenting.
Straight she ran back to her mother,
Old Louhi, Witch and toothless creature,
And these two hurried to the water,
And there found Vainamoinen weeping,
In a grove of aspens, shivering.
His hair was flowing wildly round him,
And his lips were blue and trembling.

She led him back home to her dwelling,
And she gave him there some warming,
There by her cozy burning fire,
And then said to him: "Weep no more,
O Vainamoinen, wipe your nose,
Wizard Great of Land of Heroes!
Grieve no more, friend of the waters!
Live here with us, and be you welcome.
From our platters eat your salmon,
Feed here on the sweetest bacon,
And the small fish, most delicate."
But Vainamoinen would not eat,

Shaking his head strangely, he said:
"O Louhi, Witch, I am most grateful!
Yet I will not eat at your table,
Though toothsome and so delicate
Is the food her on your plate,
Yet the food in my own pantry,
Though it's meager, is more to me.
It is better that I dwell there,
In my own beloved harbor,
In the Land of Heroes fair,
There to pour the cool, clear water
In birchen cups, from a stone pitcher,
Than in strange lands to quaff and swirl
Rich drink from a golden bowl."

"What will you give?" the Witch said then,
"Say, O ancient Vainamoinen,
If I carry you back again,
To the Land of Heroes again?"

"If you will take me across the sky
To where silver-voiced cuckoos cry,
I'll give you a helmet full of gold,
And silver, more than you could hold."

"Surely you are a wise and true
O Vainamoinen!" then said Louhi,
Scratching her chin-hair craftily.
"But I don't want your silver or gold:
I want the Sampo that you forged,
With its intricate, colored lid
And the many pictures crafted,
Made from the tip of white swan's wing,
From magic milk of virtue's song,
From the barley's finest grain,
From the wool of lambkins fine!
If you can make me the Sampo,
I give my lovely daughter to you,
The lovely Maiden of the Rainbow,
To go with you to Land of Heroes,
There to hear the silver-voiced cuckoos."

"I cannot forge the Sampo for you
With its lid of many colors,"
So answered Vainamoinen.
"If you take me to my own home,
I will send the Wizard Blacksmith,
Ilmarinen, to your service,

He, the man of mighty muscle.
He who wields the Heavy Hammer.
He will forge the Sampo clever,
Beat its lid of many colors.
He alone can win the small hand
Of the lovely Rainbow Maiden!"

"I will give my darling daughter
Only to the Sampo forger,"
Said the old Witch to the Wizard.
"Go, send Ilmarinen back here."
Then she hitched a Magic Horse
To her snow-white sledge of birches,
Placed the ancient Vainamoinen
On the sledge, to ride the north wind,
This is how she sent him homeward
To the land of mighty Wizards.
And as he raced there onward, onward,
Onward, rushing through the skies,
He heard the shuttle crack, and whiz,
He heard the mocking of her voice!
Lifting his eyes he saw her there,
On a rainbow over the water,
He saw the beautiful Rainbow Maiden,

Lovelier than a dream of heaven,
Dressed in a gold and silver air-gown.
Merrily flew a golden shuttle
In the Maid's hands to and fro,
Weaving a web of finest texture,
Combing the fringe with comb of silver.
And she mocked at the Great Wizard,
As she rustled the silver comb there,
She mocked him with her wondrous beauty,
As he rode past her in the sky,
Mocked with words of song and laughter
That he did not forget soon after.

Down the long Golden Days, returning,
Vainamoinen, in his mourning,
Thought bitterly on the Rainbow Maiden
And her mocking, maddening, taunting.
As he drove on across the hills,
He snapped his whip adorned with jewels,
Urged on faster his racing steed
So the snow-sledge creaked and rattled,
Sped like lightning through the dark fens,
Through the forests, hills and mountains,
Down the valleys, over the marshes,

Through plains and meads, and reeds and rushes,
Until at last he came again,
To the Land of Heroes and real men.
When he arrived, the Wizard began
To sing real Magic Incantation.

He sang a giant Fir Tree high,
Till it grew up and pierced the sky,
With golden branches out it reached,
Its shining limbs spread far and wide.

Then Vainamoinen sang so high,
He sang the moon into the tree,
He sang the stars, Great Bear's haunches
Tangled in the tall tree branches.
He sang his steed from tail to nose,
Home again to heather-clad meadows
Safe there in the Land of Heroes.

Now that he was home again,
He raced his sled to Ilmarinen,
And at the smithy, smoky and black,
Halted his sledge around in back.

He heard the breaking of the coal,
The roar of bellows, like a bull;
Blows of the heavy Magic Hammer.
So did the Great Wizard enter,
And there found Ilmarinen beating
His copper hammer pounding, pounding.
"Welcome, Brother, please come in!"
So said swarthy Ilmarinen.
"Why have you been gone so long?
Where on earth have you been hiding?"

"Many dreary days a-wandering,"
Answered Vainamoinen, frowning,
"Floating on the opal oceans,
Weeping in the fens and woodlands.
I visited the northern folk
And they are full of clever magic.
Up there it was a lovely Maiden,
Refused the hand of Vainamoinen,
Refused the hand of many Heroes.
All the north still sings her praises.
From her temple streams the moonlight,
From her breast shines out the sunlight,
From her forehead shines a rainbow.

On her neck, a-sparkling out so,
You can find of stars a halo!
Ilmarinen, see her, go!
See her robes of silver and gold!
At her loom, you see her seated,
On a rainbow bright and colored,
Walking about on a purple cloud!
If you will forge the Sampo for her,
With its lid of many colors,
You can win her: bring to your house,
To your smithy, a bride and spouse!"

"I know you, crafty Vainamoinen!"
Shouted trusting Ilmarinen.
"You have already promised me
To the maiden up in the sky,
To that witch, Louhi, as your gamble
To get your own self out of trouble!
I will not go to see the Maiden.
I will never live in a cavern,
Where people eat their own children!"

"I tell a greater wonder, even!"
Said the crafty Vainamoinen.

"I saw a lofty wondrous Fir Tree
With golden summit in the far sky.
I, Vainamoinen sang so high,
I sang the moon into the tall tree,
I sang the stars, the Great Bear's haunches
All tangled in the tall tree branches."

"I won't believe your crafty story,"
Cried Ilmarinen, in his smithy,
"Unless you show me that tall tree!"
"Come with me, and I will show it,"
Said Vainamoinen to the blacksmith.
Quickly they went out to see it;
Ilmarinen strode before it.
On high, he spied the glittering star,
The gleaming moonlight all entangled
In the branches far overhead.
"Climb the tree, O Ilmarinen!"
So made the challenge, Vainamoinen.
"Bring down the golden moonshine here,
And all the stars that make the Bear!"
Ilmarinen climbed up straightway,
Climbed and climbed the golden Fir Tree,
Till he came into the clouds there,

Then Vainamoinen, like quicksilver,
Sang his Magic Song of power,
So did the Wizard make his visions,
Songs and Magic Incantations,
Called the Storm Wind with this summons:
The Storm Wind blew, the Storm Wind rang,
Blowing fiercely through the sky, sang:

> *Take, O Storm Wind, Ilmarinen!*
> *In thy boat, O Wind, convey him,*
> *In thy skiff, O Wind, remove him,*
> *Quickly carry hence the Wizard,*
> *To the dark and dreary northland,*
> *To the gloomy Witch's-Haunt-Land.*

And the Storm Wind darker, darker,
Made a boat of its clouds up there.
The clouds enfolded Ilmarinen,
And sailed with him past land and ocean,
Far to the north, fast and furious,
In his cloud-boat, dark and perilous;
Ilmarinen sweeping onward,
Through the dark sky, ever northward,
Till he alighted near the woods-house,

Of Louhi, the Old-Witch-Dwelling-Place.

Overjoyed, she came to meet him.
She led him inside, and seated him
At the well-filled oaken table,
And he ate there till he was full.
After she fed him, then she said:
"O Blacksmith, Ilmarinen, Wizard,
Master of smithies, and all they do!
Can you forge the Magic Sampo,
With its lid of many colors
And its face of many pictures,
From the tips of white swan's wing-plumes,
From the magic milk of virtue,
From the single grain of barley,
From the finest lambkins' wool?
If so, I will give her to you,
Whom to see all men will love so,
Loveliest bride of any human,
My Daughter, the Rainbow Maiden."

"Yes!" replied then Ilmarinen.
"I will forge the Magic Sampo
With its lid of many colors

And its face of many pictures."

Then Ilmarinen, mighty smith,
Hastened to set up his smithy
On a rocky promontory.
He built a fire and made a chimney.
He laid his bellows, built a furnace,
In the furnace put white swan's plumes,
Put the magic milk of virtue,
Put a single grain of barley,
And the finest lambkins' wool.
Many wondrous forms of beauty,
In the fire from day to day,
All these shone within the furnace:
A golden crossbow with the brightness
Of moonbeams on the ocean's wide breast,
A purple skiff with copper oars,
A heifer with long golden horns,
A plow, with blades of molten silver.

But all these things that he made there
Were evil-borne and made great trouble;
Ilmarinen made them rubble,
Cast them back into the fire,

Burned and turned them into vapor.
On the third day, by the bellows,
Ilmarinen, bending low,
Looked into the glowing furnace
And he saw the Magic Sampo
With its lid of many colors.
Quickly with his tongs he drew it
Out of the fire, and blew on it,
And beat and forged it on his anvil,
Made his Magic Hammer flail it.

So was forged the Magic Sampo.
And it began to grind out treasure,
Wealth for the Witch, beyond measure:
From one side, it ground out fine flour,
White crystal salt came from its other,
From a third side, glittering money.
The old Witch watched it joyfully;
She grasped the Sampo in her hand,
And watched it grind and grind and grind.
She took it out east of the sun,
And hid it in a copper mountain,
And laid nine locks upon its cave,
So none but she its yield would have.

Then Ilmarinen claimed his bride,
He took the lovely Rainbow Maid,
Saying "I have forged the Sampo.
Come with me now, wherever we go!"

But she mocked him with her laughter,
Singing about the Sun's own daughter,
Till he stood with bowed head, dejected,
Full of shame, all disrespected.
Then the old Witch, Mother of craft,
Put him into a copper boat.
She sang the North Wind to her help.
The North Wind, he came roaring up,
And blew the copper boat far away,
To the Land of Heroes, the smithy,
The heather-clad meadow by the bay.

Ilmarinen, in his grieving,
Sees his wife forever, leaving,
Laughing at his swarthy skin,
Rejoicing in his look of pain.
So Ilmarinen takes his Hammer,
Blows till the fire starts to glimmer,

And gathers strength back to his heart,
For now must he attempt to craft
A new wife out of gold and silver,
One who will stay with him forever.
Seven days and nights he labors,
Till she arises from the embers.
He pulls her forth from smoke and steam,
Cools her in the mountain stream,
Polishes her to a fine gleam,
And sits admiring his handiwork,
As the day turns slowly dark.

In the night, there by the bay,
He sees his golden wife suddenly
As something hard and cold and gray.

Dismayed, he tries to have her wed
To **Vainamoinen** instead,
But the old sage just shakes his head,
Saying that the golden woman
Ought to be cast back whence she came,
And so he tells Ilmarinen:
"Throw her back in until she melts,
And forge from her a thousand trinkets."

Then he declares to all of his people,
How they may escape such trouble:

"Every child of the North, now listen,
Whether poor, or fair of fortune:
Never bow before a figure
Born of molten gold and silver:
Never while the sunlight brightens,
Never while the moonlight glimmers,
Choose a maiden made or crafted,
Choose a bride from gold created!
Cold the lips of the golden maid,
And silver breathes the breath of greed."

Epilogue:

The Death of the Sun's Daughter.

Near the door of the turf hut,
The Sun's daughter sat in silence,
Tired of the burden of her life,
Yearning, to go to another place;

Wishing for a god, a master,
A mighty god, a loving master,
A thunder-speaking foe of giants
To bring her to the Sun, her father.

She waited for the spirit death,
In the turf hut, in her sadness,
She who captured the wild reindeer
And gave them to the Sun's children.

On the last journey she will take,
Her son stands there beside her bed;

At the foot of the bed, the girl,
Young daughter of the goddesses.

The Sun's beautiful daughter speaks:
She's hard to hear, her voice is weak:
Hear her words, and remember them!
The Sun's beautiful daughter says:

"The Sun is setting, night is coming;
Night is coming, the Sun is setting;
Darkness covers the lovely people;
Morning will come, will it not come?

The sun slowly sinks, the wolf comes;
Slinks around in the dark of night;
Wily the wolf, when it's hunting,
Morning will come, will it not come?

The sun is setting, the herd shrinks,
The plague rages, insects torment,
Children grope about in the dark,
Morning will come, will it not come?

The sun sinks low, withdraws its light,
I, the Sun's daughter, see father;
I take with me, too, my own children;
Morning will come, will it not come?"

God Wears Many Skins

An Exploration of the Spiritual Basis for Sustainable Living

God Wears Many Skins

For the past twenty years, I have been engaged in rewriting religious and spiritual texts so that they better lend themselves to an ecstatic expression, as song, or poetry in recitation.

In time, my areas of interest, the texts I have chosen to make into long poems, have defined themselves as five categories:

- First, texts from Christian canon (a story of God on earth);
- Second, early texts rejected from the Christian canon (alternative stories of God on earth);
- Third, writings of fourteenth century Anglican mystics (how the individual Christian appears before God);
- Fourth, texts from other religious and folkloric traditions (how other groups might appear before God);
- and Fifth, texts relating to the Universal Declaration of Human Rights, proclaimed by the United Nations in 1948 (how ethical living may be commonly understood by all people on earth).

I believe that truth can be found in the most perfect expression. If a way of saying can be found that is more beautiful, it brings the expression closer to the truth. I also believe that all manifestations of truth converge into one truth which is the same truth for all: this means that religious, scientific, practical, esthetic truths are all the same.

If the Christian gospel texts are the actual language of God, then certainly God intends us to regard the incarnate God-man-spirit as fallible. By that, I mean capable of learning. This is shown in the episode from the Gospel of Mark where Jesus learns from his mistake:

From Mark, Chapter 7:

> There came a woman to be blessed
> Whose little daughter was possessed.
> The woman fell down at his feet,
> And begged him, cast the devil out.
> This woman, she was not a Jew;
> He wondered what he ought to do,
> And said, My children must be fed,
> Before I'd throw the dogs their bread.
> She answered, This is true, and yet
> Even the dogs some crumbs will get.
> So Jesus drove the devil out.

(Would you rather have some more "official" version of this story? Here it is, from the American Standard Version of the New Testament. "And from thence he arose, and went away into the borders of Tyre and Sidon. And he entered into a house, and would have no man know it; and he could not be hid. But straightway a woman, whose little daughter had an unclean spirit, having heard of him, came and fell down at his feet. Now the woman was a Greek, a Syrophoenician by race. And she besought him that he would cast forth the demon out of her daughter. And he said unto her, Let the children first be filled: for it is not meet to take the children's bread and cast it to the dogs. But she answered and saith unto him, Yea, Lord; even the dogs under the table eat of the children's crumbs. And he said unto her, For this saying go thy way; the demon is gone out of thy daughter. And she went away unto her house, and found the child laid upon the bed, and the demon gone out.")

Also from the Gospel of Matthew, we learn that we are all equally prone to allowing our earthly concerns to impede our spiritual belonging to God:

From Matthew, Chapter 6:

> *"I tell you, do not fret about your life,*
> *Wherefrom will come your food and what you drink,*
> *Or how your body finds what it will wear.*
> *Is not life more than what you eat and drink,*
> *And your body more than what it wears?*
> *Consider the birds, flying across the sky:*
> *They neither sow nor reap nor gather sheaves,*
> *And yet your heavenly Father finds their food.*
> *Are you not of greater worth than they?*
> *And can your worry add a single hour*
> *To the span of life that God appoints you?*
> *Consider the lilies, flourishing in the field,*
> *They neither toil nor spin, yet I tell you*
> *Even Solomon in all his glory*
> *Was never clothed as rich as one of these.*
> *If God so clothes the grasses of the field,*
> *Which are alive today and dead tomorrow,*
> *Will He not clothe you, you of little faith?*
> *Therefore do not agitate and struggle,*

> *For God knows that you need all of these things.*
> *Strive first for God, and for his righteousness,*
> *And what you need to wear and eat will follow.*
> *And do not worry what will come tomorrow;*
> *Tomorrow will bring worries of its own,*
> *And evils met today are quite sufficient."*

In this advice, Jesus warns them against the anxieties and struggles they seem condemned to impose upon themselves. How can they get past these limitations? We read in the Gospel of John that we must spiritually take ourselves all the way back to our own beginning and start over:

From John, Chapter 4:

> Jesus said to Nicodemus,
> *"Unless you're born again,*
> *You will not ever see God's face,*
> *Nor enter into heav'n."*

> But Nicodemus said to him,
> "Now my old age has come.
> Shall I then come a second time
> Into my mother's womb?"

> Jesus said, *"Unless you're born,*
> *Of water and the spir't,*
> *You will not enter into heav'n,*
> *And see the truth of it;*
> *All of these things born of the flesh*

> *Are flesh; they waste away.*
> *The things that come from the spirit*
> *You have eternally.*
>
> *So do not marvel that I said,*
> *'You must be born anew,'*
> *The wind wanders where'er it wills*
> *And comforts me, and you.*
>
> *You don't know where the wind comes from,*
> *Or where the wind will go;*
> *And so it is of ev'ry one*
> *Who has faith as I do."*

Notice that in this passage Jesus makes reference to a process of nature, the wind blowing, to express the essential motion of his (our) spiritual world. I take this to mean that we must be radically reborn in order to perceive nature as a part of us, and we a part of it. This being radically reborn may turn many things on their heads. Certainly, for women, and other oppressed classes of humanity, there is an association between the arrival of Jesus and a leveling, or upsetting, of ownership and privilege in human affairs:

From Luke, Chapter 1:

> "My whole being praises the Lord,"
> Mary sang with tears in her eyes,
> "My spirit rejoices in God,
> Who treasures my humilities;
> So now throughout all future time

> People will know this mystery:
> Holy and mighty is God's name
> Who has done all these things for me.
>
> God's mercy flows from age to age,
> With a strong arm God's will is done,
> God scatters the proud in their rage,
> Their heart's imagination gone.
>
> God overthrows these mortal kings,
> Exalting those of low degree;
> God fills the hungry with good things,
> And sends the rich empty away.
>
> As God protects all believers,
> May we remember the mercy
> That God has showed to our forebears,
> And keep God's faith eternally."

This expression of God's intention is not incidental, it is fundamental to the nature of the God which is being made incarnate in Jesus, as it is here expressed by another daughter of man:

From the *Book of Judith* (Apocrypha):

> *O Lord, your might   issues not from strong men,*
> *And your pow'r is not   by a multitude giv'n;*
> *But you are the God   of th' afflicted and weak,*
> *Helper of th' oppressed, those who weep and seek,*

> *Th' upholder and protector   of all the forlorn,*
> *The savior of them   that hope has forsworn.*

I believe the message of Jesus is that we should ferret out and reconcile all the human-imposed and worldly limitations of our language and consciousness. There was ample advice to do this, in writings which were systematically expunged from the Christian canon, by Roman church figures who wanted the authority of the church to take precedence over the potential for argumentation that might supplant its power.

Here is an example of this radical thinking, taken from *The Gospel of Thomas*, which is a "sayings collection" of the words of Jesus, presenting an account of his life by inference and without any reference to his death and resurrection.

> Jesus saw some babies nursing.
> He said to his disciples, this saying:
> "These nursing babies are like those souls
> Who enter into my Father's halls."
>
> They said to him,
> "Then shall we enter the Father's halls,
> Even though we are grown, yet as babies?"
>
> Jesus said to them,
> "When you make the two into one,
> When what is inside, outside has gone,
> And when the out is like to the in,
> And the upper like to the lower,

> All the same, seed, root and flower,
> And when you make male and female
> Into one, combining them all,
> So that the male will not be male,
> Nor will the female be female,
> When you make eyes in place of eyes,
> When you make hands in place of hands,
> A foot in place of a foot appears,
> An image in place of an image is,
> Then you will enter the Father's halls."

The gist of this kind of discourse seems to be that since God is everything, we can find and understand God better by posing and reconciling oppositions in the world and in our thinking. Here is another example from *Thunder, Perfect Mind,* a poem from the "Gnostic" tradition, found among the Nag Hammadi documents:

> Do not be arrogant to me
> When I am cast out upon the earth,
> And you will find me in those that are to come.
> And do not look upon me on the dung-heap,
> Nor go and leave me cast out,
> And so you will find me, in the kingdoms.
> And do not look upon me when I am cast out
> Among those who are disgraced
> And in the least places,
> And do not laugh at me.
> And do not cast me out
> Among those who are slain in violence.

> For I, I am compassionate, and I am cruel.
> Be on your guard!
> Do not hate my obedience,
> And do not love my self-control.
> In my weakness, do not forsake me,
> And do not be afraid of my power.

From time to time in Christian history, there have appeared people who wanted to recreate this type of opposition and reconcile it for themselves, in their own lives. This reconciliation takes place in the solitary theater of the mind of the mystic.

From *The Fire of Love*, by Richard Rolle:

> The human soul felt nothing of the burning
> Of the endless love of Jesus Christ,
> Which, before this, had not perfect forsaken
> All worldly vanity and love of opulence,
> Studying busily only heavenly things,
> Thirsting for God's love, and never ceasing,
> And mannerly loving creatures to be loved.
> For truly if we love all things in God,
> We love the God in them, more than love them;
> So not in them, but all in God we joy,
> Whom to enjoy we shall be glad always.
> The wicked truly love things of this world,
> Setting within their lust, their delectation;
> And without ceasing do the wicked covet
> Things that belong to this world's errant joy;

> How may a person do a love more fondly,
> More wretchedly, or in the ending, damnably,
> Than fully to love, and seek for themselves only,
> These transitory, ripe and failing things?

And if we do withdraw so from the world and worldliness, how does God then find us and we find God? This relationship is described by Julian of Norwich as both completely dependent and completely interdependent; she sees Jesus as our Mother who is both wrapped in the flesh of our hearts, and simultaneously, enwraps us as the Mother's womb enwraps the child; from whom we are endlessly being born, yet from whom we are never severed.

From *The Showing (The Revelation) of Love*, by Julian of Norwich:

> He wills that we be as a child,
> As when it is pained, or afraid,
> Runs hast'ly to the Mother's arms
> And may do no more than make tears,
> Crying for help with all its might.
> ...
> For when God knitted him to us
> As child within the Maiden's womb,
> He took himself our sensual soul,
> In which taking, he wrapped himself,
> Having us all enclosed in him,
> He oned himself in our substance.
> In which oneing was perfect human.
> For Christ, having knit into him
> Each and all those who shall be saved,

> Is perfect man and perfect woman.
> ...
> Thus our Lady is our Mother,
> In whom we are all like enclosed,
> And of her we are born in Christ,
> For she who's Mother of our Savior
> Is mother of all who shall be saved;
> And our Savior our very Mother,
> In whom we are endlessly born
> Yet never shall come out of him.

This form of dynamic interdependence is characteristic of animistic religious systems such as that of the Sami, indigenous people of Northern Europe and Asia. They believe that the sun (male) and the earth (female) mated to make a son, who then found a bride and fathered human beings. The earth and sun share our experience of living, as do all plant and animal creatures:

From *How the Bear Speaks to God*, Sami folklore:

> The Sami tell how we began
> here on this world that's always been:
> Our life, born of the father Sun
> And the mother Earth under him.
> So have men and women been born
> Since the son of the Sun returned.
> They have this world in equal share
> With reindeer, fish, fox, wolf and bear;
> All animals and folk belong

> To the same source and becoming.
> They are all linked by their spirits
> And none of them holds dominance.
>
> Those who believe only one God
> Made every thing that is good,
> Think of God as something they own.
> The Sami see, God wears many skins:
> The Sami do not care who owns:
> They do not force others to bow:
> All the other views may be true.

The intimate, reciprocal involvement of all life forms, even of what Christian cultures may regard as "the inanimate," both reduces the sense of human entitlement, and substantiates a subconscious respect for our "environment." We have not segregated a class of lesser things or animals for contempt, consumption or disposal.

From *The Navajo Creation Story*:

> The Gods laid one of the buckskins
> Flat and smooth upon the sandstones,
> Careful that its head faced the west.
>
> On that buckskin they lay two ears,
> Side by side there as companions,
> So that the tips are pointed east.

Then the Gods laid the other buckskin
Smooth over the two ears of corn,
Careful that its head faced the east.

Then the Gods, under the white ear,
They put a big white eagle's feather;
And told the people to stand back.

Then they, under the yellow ear,
Put a yellow eagle's feather;
And told people again, stand back.

Then from the east the White Wind blew,
Between the skins, all the way through,
While all the people stood and looked.

And while the wind came around them,
Each of the Holy People came,
Around the corn and skins they walked.

Four times they walked around this bed,
And the two feathers tips protruded,
And ever so slightly, they moved.

When the Holy Ones were all done
Walking around their construction,
They lifted the topmost buckskin.

Look! The ears of corn disappeared!

> There in their place there had appeared
> A new man and a new woman!

Even in spiritual systems that avoid mention of deities, this type of interdependence is perceived as virtuous. In one of the most ancient of these, Confucius advises us to reconcile with the parts of our world that are most different from what we think we want, in his commentary in the Second Image of the *Book of Change*:

> Because your goodness is virtue,
> It supports what all others do.
>
> Support of virtue is felt most
> By them who have some virtue lost.
>
> Therefore you should be more humane
> With inhumanity and sin.
>
> Only the humane support all people
> And not just those they may resemble.
>
> Have courage to like and dislike,
> And the strength to keep coming back.
>
> Those who love their own families
> Also love their dogs and horses.
>
> Without respecting difference,
> Can we say they have any friends?

> Sometimes the outcast does the work
> That the privileged one would shirk;
>
> And at the family dinner,
> The first dish is for grandfather;
>
> If we observe such customs well,
> A humane virtue supports it all.

Climate change, however, is not a problem to be solved just by an individual Christian, or mystic, or a person from any particular religious tradition. It applies as an ethical and practical matter equally to everybody on earth. What kind of spiritual canon or statement would address people from this viewpoint? The closest thing we have is a document originally engendered in 1948 by the United Nations, the *Universal Declaration of Human Rights*. It doesn't exactly say that human beings have the right to be free from climate change, but covers the need by inference:

> Article 22: Everyone, as a member of society, has the right to social security and is entitled to realization, through national effort and international co-operation and in accordance with the organization and resources of each State, of the economic, social and cultural rights indispensable for his dignity and the free development of his personality.

I think that in order for us to realize these rights, we have think globally and act locally. This means, we have to assume that every newborn baby starts with an equal complement of rights which are then to a greater or lesser degree eroded by societies, governments and the like. The Declaration as much as says so, in Article 1:

> All human beings are born free and equal in dignity and rights. They are endowed with reason and conscience and should act towards one another in a spirit of brotherhood.

This is where we should be mindful:

> Every baby is born free,
> Each one is born in dignity.
> Sons and daughters, all the same,
> Every baby has a name.
> Each one has a power of thought,
> Which cannot be sold or bought,
> And a conscience, every one
> Which we cannot blot with pain.
> Every baby's dignity
> Creates the world for you and me,
> To see each child among the others
> Tells of the fathers and the mothers.

CPSIA information can be obtained
at www.ICGtesting.com
Printed in the USA
LVHW071050150623
749847LV00003B/220